RALSTON CRAWFORD

Cover by Ralston Crawford: *Los Penitentes,* 1973

RALSTON CRAWFORD, *New Orleans, November, 1972*
By Peggy Crawford

GRAPHICS '73
RALSTON CRAWFORD

Organized by the

UNIVERSITY OF KENTUCKY ART GALLERY
With the support of special grants from
The Kentucky Arts Commission,
The University of Kentucky,
The University of Kentucky Research Foundation

Lexington, February 11-March 4, 1973

TABLE OF CONTENTS

ACKNOWLEDGMENTS

This publication is the result of the author's third "Crawford Campaign." The first, in 1953, dealt with Ralston Crawford's paintings, the second in 1962, his lithographs, and now this one concentrates on his drawings. While it is generally true that the author gets the credit for a book, in a work of this type, the artist plays the really indispensable part, above all by being patient. He must be ready to answer innumerable questions, put up with impositions of every sort and at the same time try to keep up with the necessities of his professional career as an artist.

In this roundabout way, I am trying to thank Ralston Crawford for his enormous help in this as in the two earlier Campaigns.

At the same time I wish also to thank the Kentucky Arts Commission, the University of Kentucky Research Foundation and President Otis A. Singletary of the University of Kentucky for making possible the publication of "Graphics '73—Ralston Crawford," the 15th in the annual series devoted to facets of contemporary graphic arts.

Individuals by the score have assisted at one time or another, to a greater or lesser degree, and in every case importantly. Certainly James Edgy, Executive Director of the Kentucky Arts Commission, Dr. James S. Pierce, Dr. Lewis W. Cochran, Dean Art Gallaher, Jr., Jo Leadingham and Vi Kiviniemi should be singled out for special thanks.

The generosity of the lenders to the exhibition, which include institutions as well as individuals and whose names are recorded elsewhere, is hereby acknowledged. We are deeply indebted to them for their crucial help.

Dr. Joshua Taylor, Director, Janet Flint, Curator of Prints, and Harry Lowe, Director of Exhibits, at the National Collection of Fine Arts of the Smithsonian Institution, have each at one time or another given vital support and encouragement. Thanks to them "Graphics '73—Ralston Crawford" will be seen in the print exhibition galleries at 8th and G Streets in Washington, D.C., from April 27 through May 27, 1973.

The design of this publication is by Ellsworth Taylor of the University's Printing Division to whom we are grateful for his co-operation at every stage of the production. Thanks, too, to Peggy Crawford for her photo-portrait of her husband and to Virginia Zabriskie of the Zabriskie Gallery for her generous assistance.

R.B.F.

RALSTON CRAWFORD'S DRAWINGS

"In some ways drawing seems to painting as the musical trio or quartet is to the symphony, i.e. sometimes better, but less pretentious, quieter and therefore not for many immediately arresting or captivating. So a concern with drawings calls for a special, perhaps greater cultivation."

RALSTON CRAWFORD
in a letter to the author
December 30, 1963

Ralston Crawford's drawings play a major role in his activity as an artist, and it is becoming increasingly clear to more and more people that they are no more record of places visited, or of people met, or of things seen. Their importance to him is expressed in the paragraph quoted above and manifests itself in the way he refers to his "Note Books" or "Drawing Books," never to "Sketch Books," a term which he would usually find applicable to something ill considered or roughly executed.

It is of course evident that his drawings often do record where he has been, but far more than that, in the long succession of drawings of every type over many years, they have recorded his future plans.

One can discern from a very early date the moral climate, the intellectual integrity and the increasingly personal way of communication that stamps any drawing of the last forty years as a "Crawford." They present unmistakable evidence too, that the artist has traveled under what Igor Stravinsky called the "stern auspices of order and discipline." His uniqueness was noted by Laurence Campbell in *Art News* in an exhibition of early Crawford works at the Zabriskie Gallery in New York in May, 1971:
". . . and yet everything looks as though only he could do it."

In 1947 there was an exhibition of drawings at Howard University, and "Graphics '73" is the first since then to focus on Crawford's lifetime devotion to drawing and to his watercolors, both transparent and opaque.

While the earliest post-Pennsylvania Art Academy drawings from the early 1930's are arresting examples of a discerning and perceptive young artist already in command of formidable skills in linear expression, to students of Crawford's work they reveal qualities that will contribute to the "uniqueness" mentioned above; for instance, the precision of the clapboarding of a country store, the sense of volume and geometric shapes in a barn in Exton, Pennsylvania, the concern for the pattern of the floorboards of a stage on which two unicyclists gyrate dextrously; and always that sharply focussed eye for significant aspects of a situation.

The individual stamp of "Crawford" quite clearly appears around 1937 with studies in pen and ink, sometimes with watercolor, of beach scenes or of gas tanks at Sanford, Orlando and Maitland, Florida. The drawing of a ship's cargo booms in New Orleans of the same year is unmistakably a "Crawford."

One of the remarkable things in the record since then is that it holds true for drawings of subject matter as diverse as the waterfront in Buffalo, the Atom Bomb "Test Able" at Bikini Atoll, the cemeteries of New Orleans, the bullfights in Spain and the fishing boats in the harbor of Stornoway, among scores of other subjects that have captured his attention. It also holds true in motifs that range from the inch by inch observation of a freight car coupling in Minneapolis to the agonized comments on war and destruction that filled so much of his mind and so many of his works during the '40's and '50's.

No single way of drawing makes his work immediately identifiable. It ranges from simple, single line explorations, frequently taut with drama and emotion, to volumetric studies in which parallel hatching or cross-hatching lines of varying degrees of fineness are useful. Solid areas of ink or pencil or color in some others serve still another function. There are variations and combinations of all these. Paper dimensions remain modest always. The great majority are in the neighborhood of a generous pocket size. Some notebooks literally could fit in a vest pocket, and the drawings therein lose none of their impact. A medieval miniaturist, for instance, would admire the completeness of the statement made in an area 1⅝ x 2¼ inches (#22), a detail from the record of a visit to the wartime Curtiss-Wright plant in Buffalo.

While unique properties are undoubtedly significant in the work of any artist, the great reward in Crawford's drawings is what finally must be described as "quality". This term includes the selective eye, the economic precision of expression, the poetry of the harmonious relationships of lines, the inventiveness, the taste, the often sheer elegance of line, and so much more, too. The means vary with the statements the artist has to make. To express his vision of contemporary urban environment calls for the use of a line very different from the shattered shapes of destruction at Cologne and Bikini, or the poignancy of death in a Spanish Bull Ring. Flowing curved lines appear to be singularly appropriate for Grand Prix racing cars, as are the ruled geometric lines that might refer to aspects of building operations in lower Manhattan.

Crawford has expressed his admiration for many artists, most especially among the moderns for Cézanne, Gris and Picasso, all of whom have been important to him as a painter, all of whom share with him truly Classical characteristics. The genealogy of his drawing, it seems to this writer, goes back through Degas and Ingres, through Poussin and Piero, to Euphronios and Exekias. Its origin could very well be in ancient Egypt. His palette generally leans toward the cool side. The 17th Century Dutch master Vermeer of Delft comes to mind, but Crawford's blue is an electric blue. As Elizabeth Sacartoff of *Time* magazine and *P.M.*, the old New York daily, remarked over thirty years ago, his is "a special blue, giving an effect of great speed"; his yellows also appear "special"—significantly, close to uranium salts in color, instead of Vermeer's lemon yellow. This artist is a man of today.

The vast industrial development, the cataclysmic events, the fantastic increase in tempo, the shrinking of space, the new problems that trouble our time seem recorded in Crawford's art with the precision of a seismograph. With his remarkable range of interests and enthusiasms he would insist that the cave paintings at Ajanta in India, the austerity of the landscape and the fishing fleets of the Outer Hebrides, the bullfights and the church festivals of Spain, the jazz musicians and the cemeteries of New Orleans have all had their impact. Perhaps here, or nearby, there could be references to Catalonian art in the museum in Barcelona; to the El Grecos, the Goyas and many others in the Prado, the National Gallery, London, and the Rijksmuseum, Amsterdam.

He recalled to me that Julius Meier-Graefe had once remarked that he went to Spain to see Velasquez and discovered El Greco. Crawford said he went to Spain to see El Greco and discovered Goya. He expresses unbounded admiration for both Goya and Rembrandt. "There's no one who can put a glove on either of them," he told me this past November.

Automobile racing, too, has long attracted him. He has often attended the great races at Le Mans, Monza, Monte Carlo, Sebring, Daytona, Watkins Glen and even the Indianapolis "500." He has spent many days and nights on the straightaways, the curves and in the pits and the infield at these tracks. He identifies with Sterling Moss and Jackie Stewart; as he does with Louis Armstrong, Sidney Bechet and George Lewis; with Ordoñez and Litri and with Armand Rousseau and Drouhin-Laroze of Gevrey-Chambertin. In sum, he respects and admires the artists in any field, be they racing drivers, jazz musicians, bull fighters or vintners of Burgundy.

He was at Bikini Atoll as a reporter for "Fortune" magazine when atomic Test Able was detonated in 1946. So that he could see the fireball and the subsequent mushroom cloud better he took off the special protective glasses he had been issued but prudently covered one eye since he had been told that there might be a temporary impairment of his vision. For many years after, his drawings recalled the implications of what he saw.

I wrote to ask him once about the subject matter of a certain drawing. His answer: "I find it impossible to answer your question. The 'subject matter' is never limited to a single visual impact or idea. Indeed it is a picture of the other pictures one has seen, of one's response to his time, one's recollection of his friends, their stimulating and enlightening remarks, or it is the smile, the handshake, the voice that may nourish us for years and will contribute to the form of the picture. This diffusion grows more complex as we continue to live. How are we to sort out such subject matter? I neither know nor care."

Historically he has been linked to a group of New York-based artists whose work is distinguished by the use of cleanly separated areas of color— the so-called "Hard Edge" or "Precisionist" painters—and by their inclination toward the subject matter of urban America. A number of them have been Crawford's close friends, George L. K. Morris, Robert Gwathmey, Niles Spencer, Stuart Davis, Louis Guglielmi, among others. Though they shared many of the same concerns, there is no evidence of any important influence of any of them on Crawford. Charles Sheeler, popularly cited for his early interest in industrial subject matter, was associated with Edith Halpert's Downtown Gallery in New York where Crawford and several of his friends exhibited, but Crawford and Sheeler had different approaches and very different gifts. There is no visible artistic connection, although a number of people have felt that at times Crawford played a strong part in the work of the older artist.

The great majority of Crawford's drawings are executed in pen and ink. There exist some in pencil, a few in pastel and a considerable number in watercolor, both transparent and gouache. The fluidity of watercolor in combination with the penned line elicits a feeling of spontaneity, even gaiety. It was used principally in the early years of his career, while gouache reflects the more studied procedure of his maturity. In many cases they are steps to major oils or lithographs. They have a striking individuality, and in spite of their small scale they occupy a distinglished place in his production.

Last October I pressed the artist further on the relative importance of his drawing to his other work. His reply eloquently sums up the reason for this exhibition:

"The drawings will, if you care to take the trip, bring you back-stage. They are the record of my inquiry, my quest. They are the expression of my most private activity in picture-making, and one of the most important expressions. They are in many cases among my best work. In any case they are the immediate source of my work in painting, lithography, motion-picture filming, still photography, and sound recording. They are basic to my design—in a total sense."

Richard B. Freeman
Lexington, Kentucky
February, 1973

CHRONOLOGY

1906	Born, September 25, at St. Catharines, Ontario.
1926-27	Sailor on tramp steamers to Caribbean, Central America and California. First trip to New Orleans. Study at Otis Art Institute, Los Angeles. Work in Walt Disney's studio.
1927-30	Study at the Pennsylvania Academy in Philadelphia and the Barnes Foundation, Merion, Pa. Awarded two scholarships.
1930-32	Painting in New York. Tiffany Fellowship.
1932-33	In Europe. Study at Academies Colarossi and Scandinave, Paris. Travel in Spain, Italy and Balearic Islands.
1933	New York. Study at Columbia University.
1934	First one-man show, Maryland Institute of Art, Baltimore. (For others, see list page 80.)
1934-39	Painting in Exton and Chadds Ford, Pennsylvania.
1937-38	Bok Fellowship, Florida. First sustained experience with photography. Trip to New Orleans.
1940	New York. Painting, book illustrations and jackets.
1940-41	Visiting Instructor, Art Academy of Cincinnati.
1942	Visiting Instructor, School of Fine Arts, Buffalo. Purchase prize for color lithograph, Metropolitan Museum of Art, New York.
1943-45	Chief of Visual Presentation Unit of the Weather Division, Headquarters, Army Air Force, Washington, D.C.
1945	Assigned to China-Burma-India theater.
1946	Awarded Army Commendation Ribbon. Eyewitness in civilian status to atomic bomb Test Able, Bikini Atoll.
1947	Guest Director, Honolulu School of Art.
1948-49	Instructor, Brooklyn Museum Art School. Visiting Instructor, Art Academy of Cincinnati and University of Minnesota.
1949-50	Visiting Artist, Louisiana State University.
1950	Photography in Mexico. Lecture tour to 28 colleges in the United States.
1950-68	Many trips to New Orleans to photograph the negro musicians principally and the life around their music.
1951-52	Travel in Europe. Intensive work in lithography in Paris. Visiting Artist, University of Colorado.
1952-57	Faculty, New School for Social Research, New York.
1953	Publication of "Ralston Crawford" by Richard B. Freeman, University of Alabama Press. Visiting Artist, University of Michigan.
1954-55	Paris, further intensive work in lithography and painting. Trip to Spain for observation of Goya's paintings and the bullfights.
1956	Lecture tour for American Association of Colleges.
1957	France, work in lithography and painting. Another trip to Spain.
1958	Visiting Artist, University of Colorado.
1959	Trip to Spain and Paris for further lithography.
1960-62	Faculty, Hofstra College.

1960   Visiting Artist, University of Kentucky and University of Southern California.

1961   Appointed Photographic Research Consultant, Tulane University, Archive of New Orleans Jazz.
Visiting Artist, University of Minnesota at Duluth.

1962   Trip to Greece, Egypt, France; lithography and photography. Publication of "The Lithographs of Ralston Crawford," by Richard B. Freeman, University of Kentucky Press.

1962-68   Frequent attendance at Grand Prix car races in Europe and the U.S.A.

1963   Trip to Scandinavia, Germany, North Africa, Ireland, Scotland.

1964   Trips to Tobago, Trinidad, Maine, Norway.

1965   Visiting Artist, Sheldon Art Galleries, University of Nebraska.

1966   Visiting Artist, University of Illinois. Trip to Ireland, Isle of Man, England, France, Germany, Denmark.

1967   England, Spain, Denmark.

1968   Trip to Guadeloupe, Martinique, Orkney and Shetland Islands.

1969   Painting in New York. Travel and painting, motion picture photography in Madrid, Seville, Tangiers, Fez, Pamplona. Shows "Various Depths" at the Creighton University Film Festival.

1970   Work in New York. To Seville for Holy Week. Recipient of cash award from National Academy of Arts and Letters: ". . . for his forthright contributions in painting and lithography, stressing the 20th century tensions between warm humanism and bleak objectivity." To Grand Coulee Dam, Washington, on behalf of Bureau of Reclamation, U.S. Department of the Interior.

1971   To Seville, Pamplona, the Outer Hebrides, London: Shows three short films: "Torn Signs," "Room 333" and "Big Bayou Black" at St. Louis Art Museum.

1972   Completes major oil "Celebration (Los Penitentes)", purchased by the Munson-Williams-Proctor Institute, Utica, N.Y. To Seville for Holy Week; later, to North Africa, Madrid, London. In New York to receive the Edwin Palmer Memorial Prize, National Academy of Design. In the summer to the Isle of Harris and Lewis in the Outer Hebrides for further drawing and work on still and moving picture film. Then to Lisbon, Madeira, Seville. Upon return to New York an intensive and productive period of painting that carries on well into 1973.

CATALOG

° Measurements are of paper size, unless otherwise noted, height first.

BLACK & WHITE DRAWINGS

1. NUDE, Exton, Pa. 1933
   Ink 9⅜ x 12½   p. 22

2. RECLINING NUDE 1934
   Ink 7½ x 10   p. 20

3. NUDE SEATED IN CHAIR 1934
   Ink 7½ x 10   p. 21

4. COMPOSITION 1935
   Crayon and pencil 7½ x 10   p. 23
   Lent by Mr. & Mrs. Maurice Vanderwoude, Great Neck, N.Y.

5. EXTON INTERIOR 1935
   Ink and crayon 13⅞ x 9¾   p. 17
   Lent by the St. Louis Art Museum

6. INDIAN RUN FARM, Exton 1936
   Ink 9¾ x 14   p. 18

7. STILL LIFE, Exton 1936
   Ink 9¾ x 14   p. 19

8. PROMENADE 1937
   Ink 11 x 17   p. 24

9. WHITE LINES ON DARK GROUND 1938
   Ink 7½ x 10   p. 26

10. SANFORD TANKS 1938
    Lithographic crayon 7½ x 10   p. 32
    Lent by Emily S. Rauh, St. Louis, Mo.

11. ORLANDO FLORIDA 1938
    Ink 9½ x 14   p. 31

12. SANFORD 1938
    Ink 11 x 17   p. 30

13. READING, PA., FAIR 1938
    Ink 8½ x 11   p. 29

14. MARKET STREET, Wilmington, Del. 1938
    Ink 10 x 7½   p. 27

15. OVERSEAS HIGHWAY 1939
    Ink and crayon 7½ x 10   p. 33
    Lent by the Greenberg Gallery, St. Louis

16. MAITLAND BRIDGE 1939
    Ink and crayon 7½ x 10   p. 35
    Lent by the Greenberg Gallery, St. Louis

17. BRIDGE NEAR EASTHAMPTON, CONN. 1939
    Ink 7½ x 10   p. 28

18. TOO MARVELOUS FOR WORDS 1940
    Ink 11 x 17   p. 25

19. ANCHOR 1941
    Ink 9½ x 12   p.36

20. A MAN IN MISPASSAGE, Nov. 28, 1943
    Ink 11½ x 14½   p. 38

21. GAS MASK 1945
    Ink 11¾ x 14½   p. 37

22. CURTISS-WRIGHT #1 1945
    Ink 11½ x 14½   p. 40

23. CURTISS-WRIGHT #2 1945 ?
    Ink 11⅝ x 14⅝   p. 41

24. THE BRIDGE (BOMBED) 1945
    Ink 14½ x 11½   p. 39

25. CRASH 1945
    Ink 14½ x 23   p. 43

26. PLANE CRASH 1945 ?
    Ink 14½ x 23   p. 44
    Lent by Department of Art, Univ. of Colorado

27. MISSION #1 1945
    Ink 14½ x 23   p. 45

28. BIKINI 1946
    Ink 14¾ x 11½   p. 42

29. DRAWING FOR "TEST ABLE" 1946
    Ink 11½ x 14½   p. 46

30. SEA PLANE TAKE-OFF AND U.S.S. NEVADA, BIKINI 1946
    Ink 7¼ x 11½   p. 47

31. BIKINI 1947
    Ink 11¼ x 14½   p. 48

32. THIRD AVENUE ELEVATED #1 1947
    Ink 9½ x 11¾   p. 52

33. THIRD AVENUE ELEVATED #2 1947
    Ink 9½ x 11¾   p. 53

34. WHARF OBJECTS AT SANTA BARBARA 1947
    Ink 11⅝ x 14¼   p. 50

35. ELEVATED c. 1948
    Ink 14½ x 11½   p. 55

36. BOXCARS, MINNEAPOLIS 1948
    Ink 11½ x 14½   p. 49

37. BOXCARS, MINNEAPOLIS 1950
    Ink 7¼ x 10   p. 51

5. *Exton Interior, 1935*

RALSTON CRAWFORD

6. *Indian Run Farm, Exton, 1936*

Ralston Crawford
EXTON, 1936

7. *Still Life, Exton, 1936*

Ralston Crawford

1934

2. *Reclining Nude, 1934*

3. *Nude Seated in Chair, 1934*

CRAWFORD
1933

1. Nude, Exton, Pa., 1933

RALSTON CRAWFORD

4. *Composition, 1935*

23

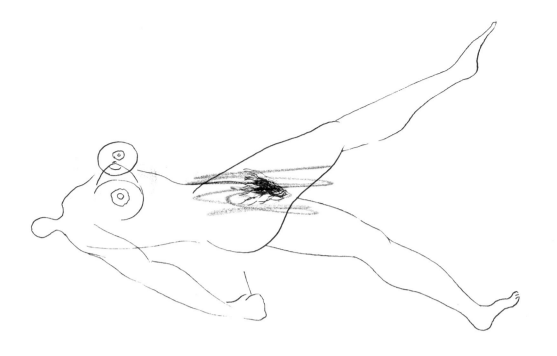

RALSTON CRAWFORD, 1937

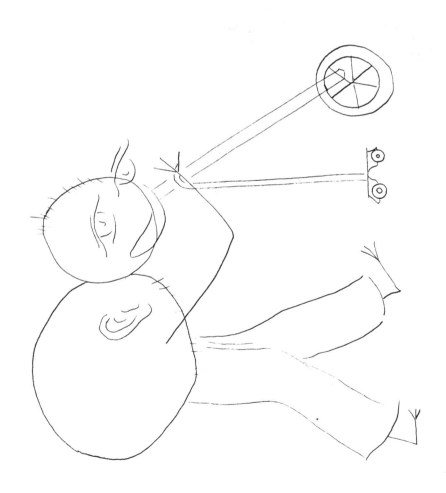

8. *Promenade, 1937*

24

RALSTON CRAWFORD
1940

18. *Too Marvelous for Words, 1940*

Ralph Crawford

1938

9. *White Lines on Dark Ground, 1938*

14. *Market Street, Wilmington, Del., 1938*

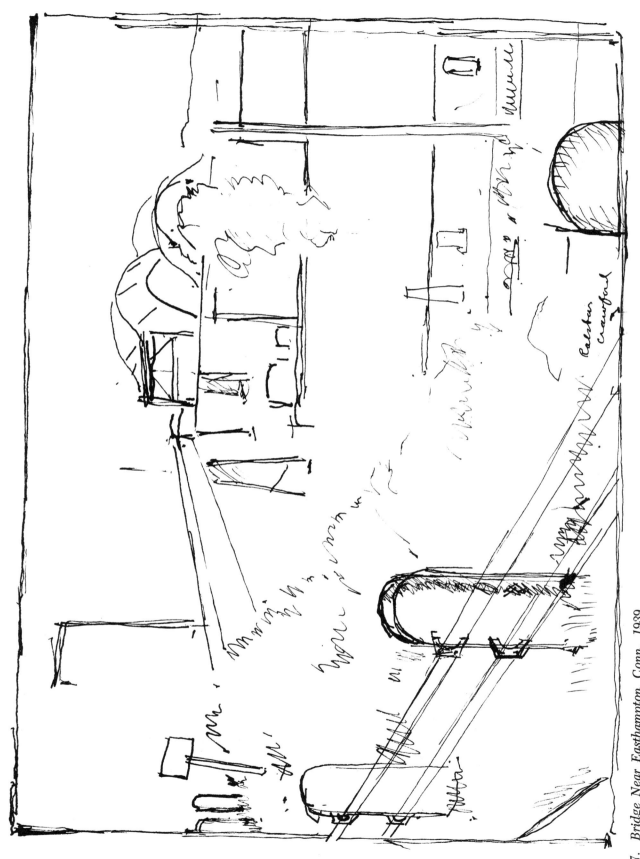

17. *Bridge Near Easthampton, Conn., 1939*

Reading, Pa.
Fair, 1938

13. *Reading, Pa., Fair, 1938*

Ralph Crawford '38

12. *Sanford, 1938*

11. *Orlando, Florida, 1938*

10. *Sanford Tanks, 1938*

Ralston Crawford

15. *Overseas Highway, 1939*

Ralph Crawford '38

62. *Maitland Bridge, 1938*

34

1939   Ralston Crawford

16. *Maitland Bridge, 1939*

35

RALSTON CRAWFORD, 1941

19. Anchor, 1941

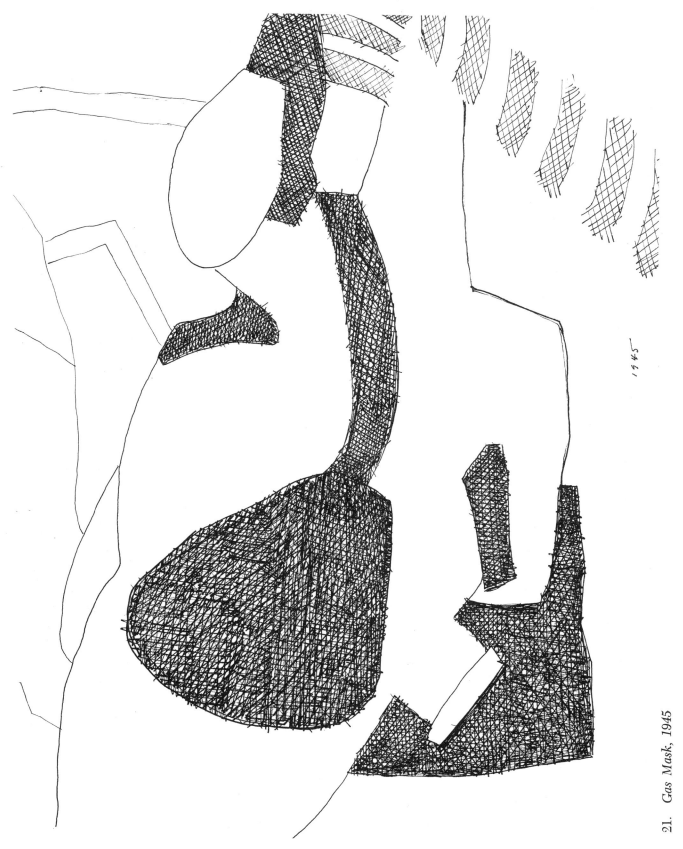

21. *Gas Mask, 1945*

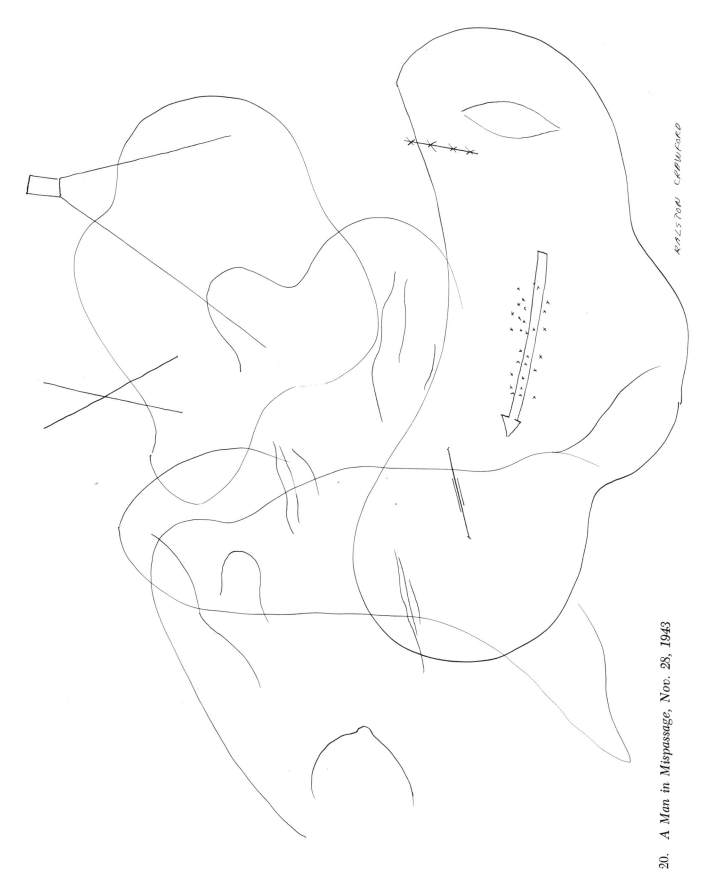

RALSTON CRAWFORD

20. *A Man in Mispassage, Nov. 28, 1943*

24.   *The Bridge (Bombed), 1945*

1945

RALSTON
CRAWFORD

22. *Curtiss-Wright #1, 1945*

RALSTON
CRAWFORD

23. *Curtiss-Wright #2, 1945 ?*

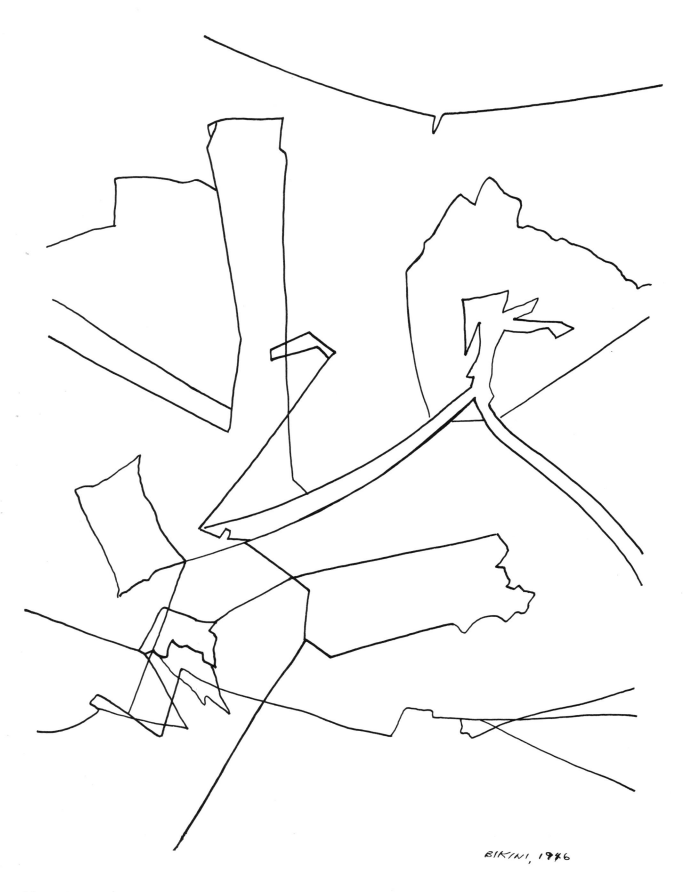

BIKINI, 1946

28. *Bikini, 1946*

Ralston Crawford '45

25. *Crash, 1945*

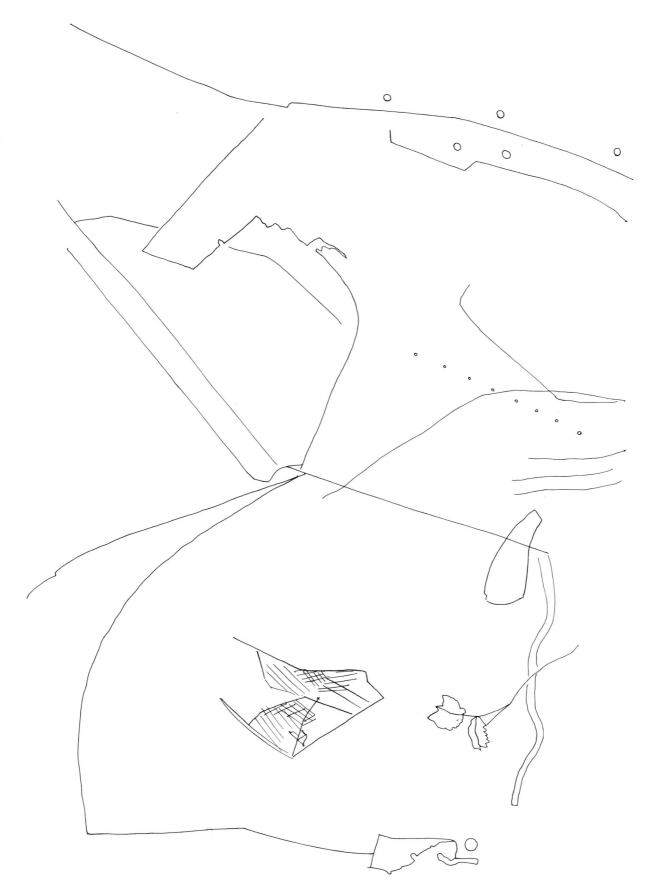

26. *Plane Crash*, 1945 ?

27. *Mission #1 1945*

29. *Drawing for "Test Able," 1946*

RALSTON
CRAWFORD

30. Sea Plane Take-off and U.S.S. Nevada, Bikini, 1946

Ralston Crawford

31. *Bikini, 1947*

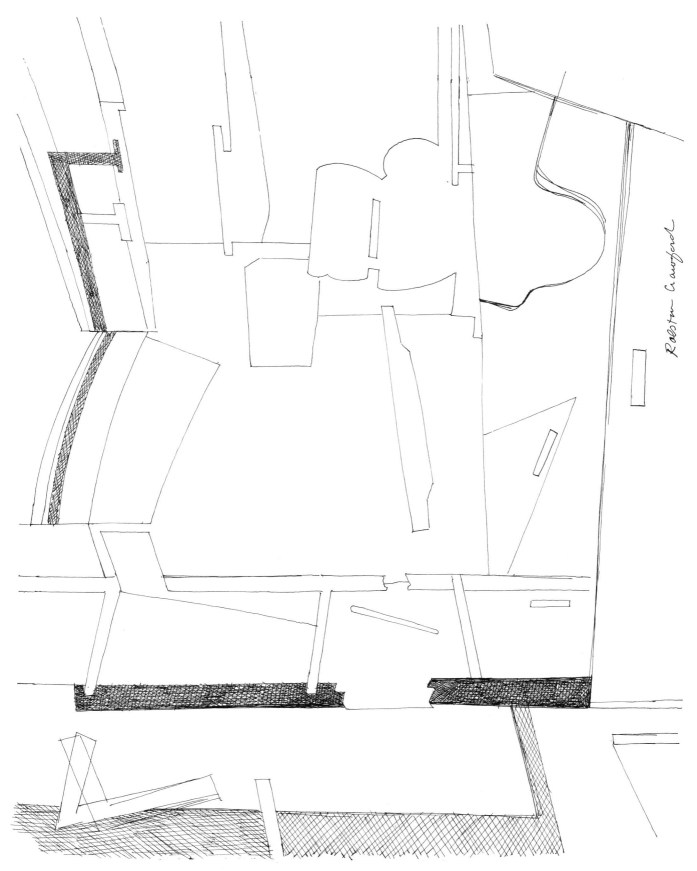

36. *Boxcars, Minneapolis, 1948*

34. *Wharf Objects at Santa Barbara, 1947*

37. *Boxcars, Minneapolis, 1950*

RALSTON CRAWFORD

1947

32. *Third Avenue Elevated #1 1947*

52

1947

RALSTON CRAWFORD

33. *Third Avenue Elevated #2, 1947*

39. *Third Avenue Elevated #3, prob. 1952*

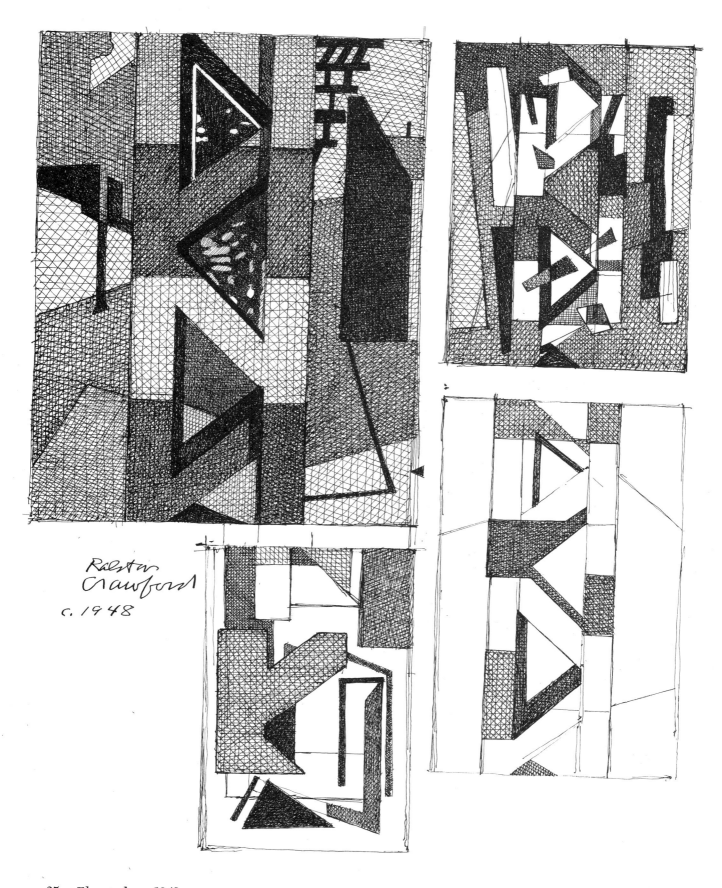

Ralston
Crawford
c. 1948

35. *Elevated, c. 1948*

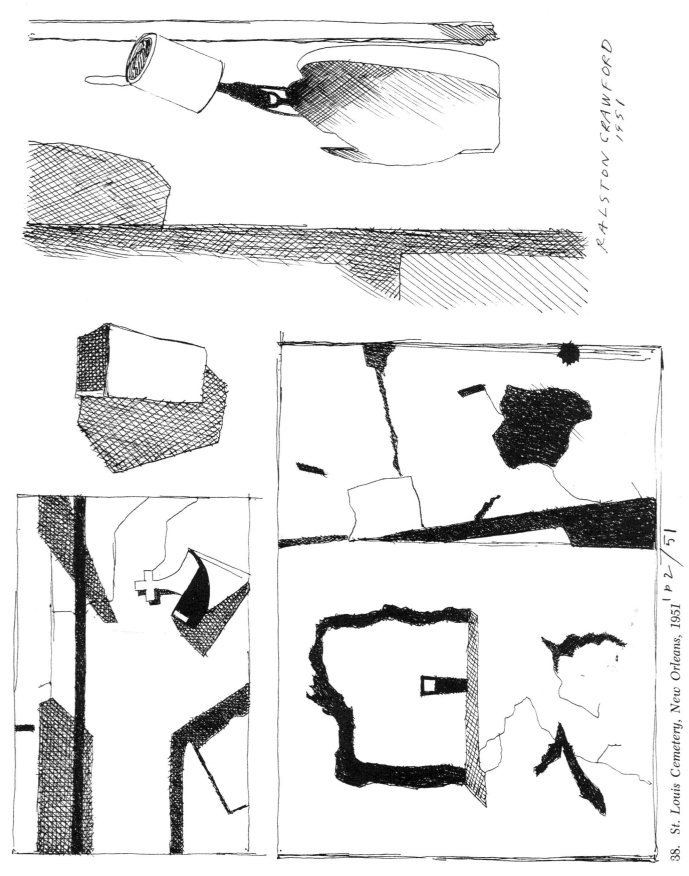

RALSTON CRAWFORD
1951

38. *St. Louis Cemetery, New Orleans, 1951*

spring. 1952   RALSTON CRAWFORD

40. Cologne, Spring, 1952

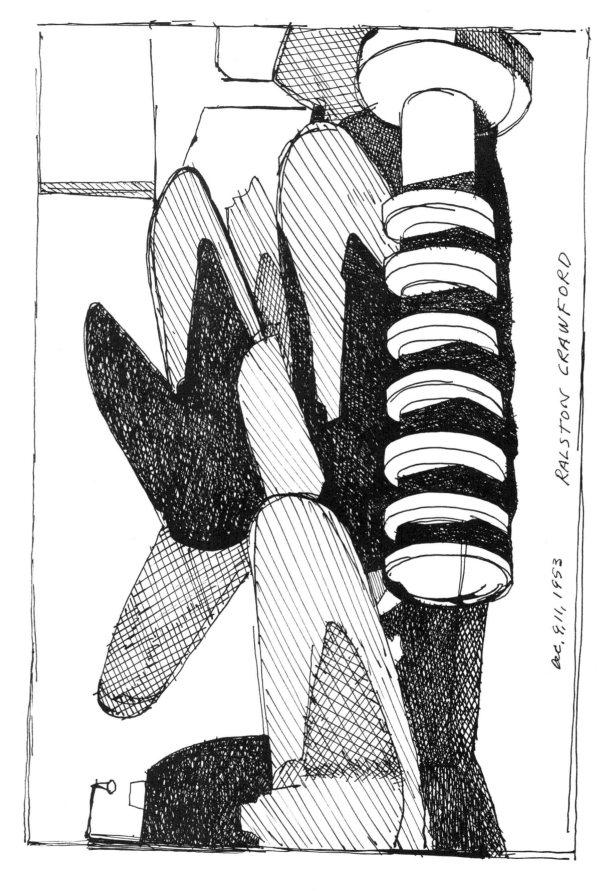

41. *Shaw's Propellors #1, Dec. 9, 11, 1953*

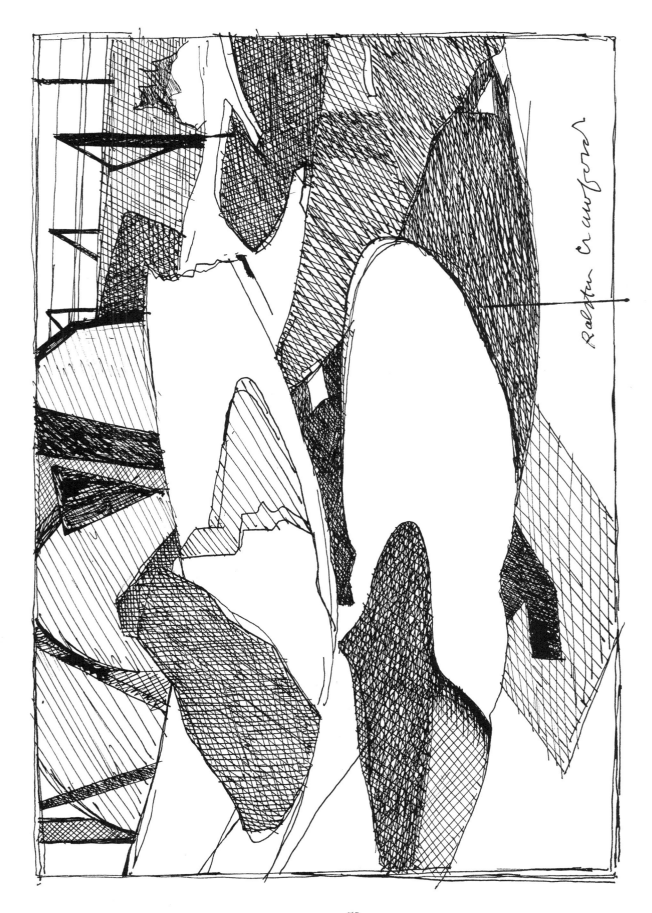

Ralston Crawford

42. *Shaw's Propellors #2, Dec. 11, 12, 15, 1953*

43. *Notebook Page, New Orleans #1, Aug. 5,*
    Oct. 6, 1953

44. *Notebook Page, New Orleans #2, Oct. 12, 1953*

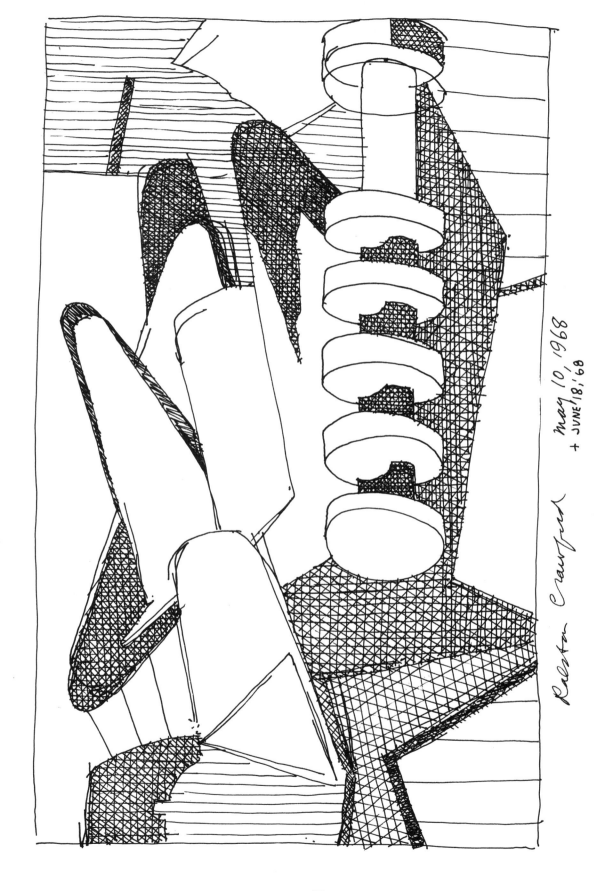

Ralston Crawford   may 10, 1968
+ June 18, '68

55. *Shaw's Propellors #3, May 10, June 18, 1968*

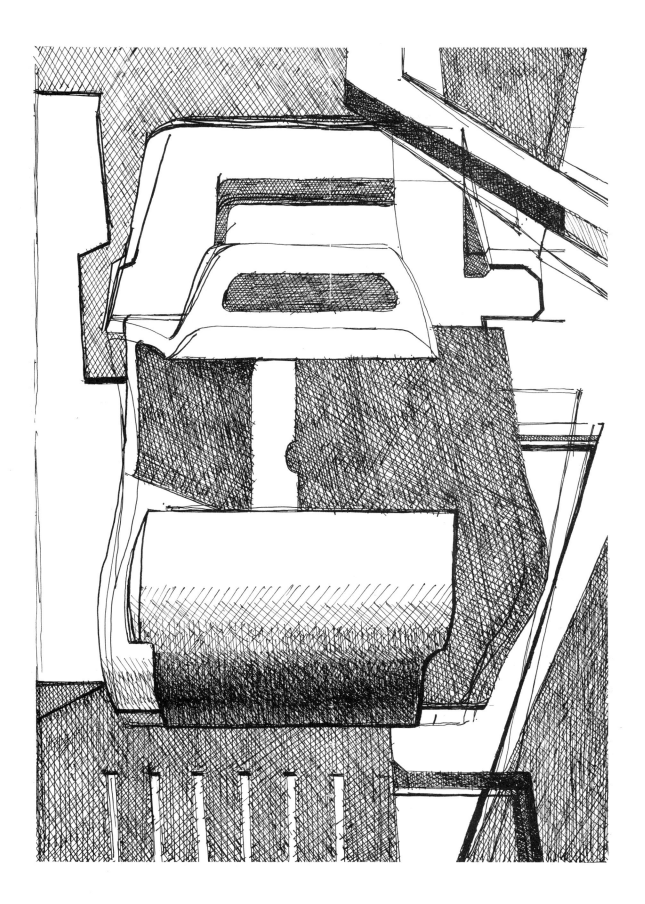

45. *Boxcar Coupling, 1954*

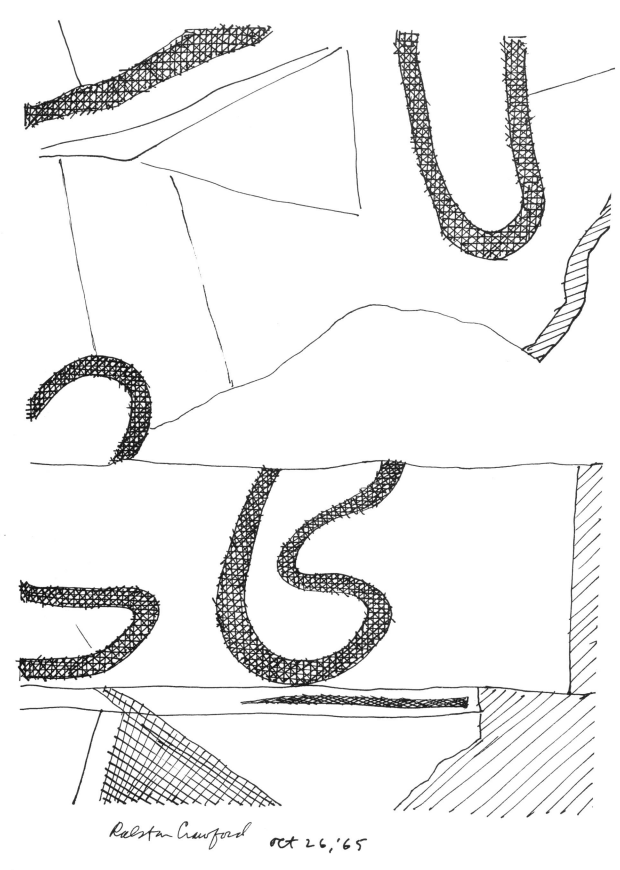

Ralston Crawford   oct 26, '65

50. *Signboards, New York #1, Oct. 26, 1965*

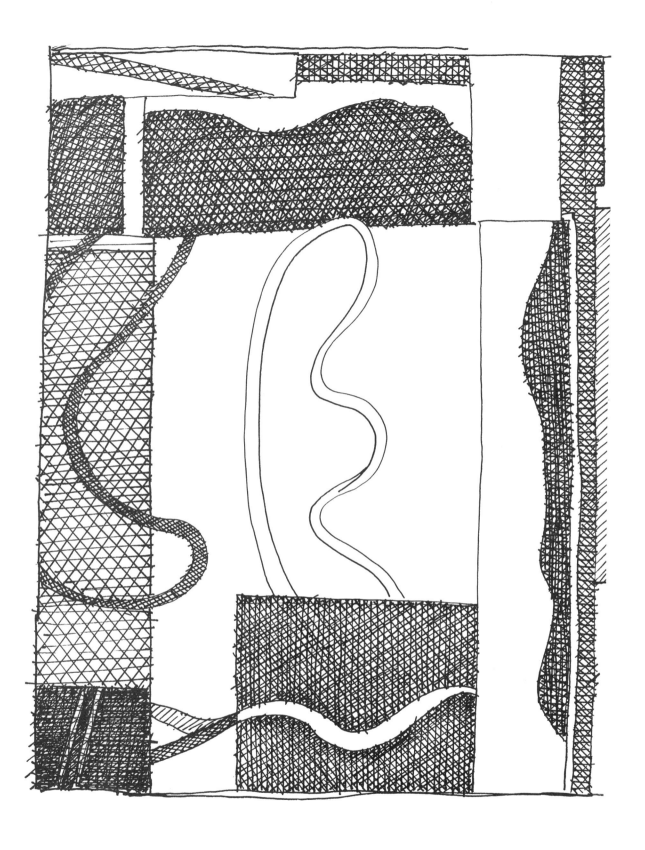

51. *Signboards, New York #2, Nov. 3, 1965*

47. *Port Clyde #1, Oct. 21, 1964*

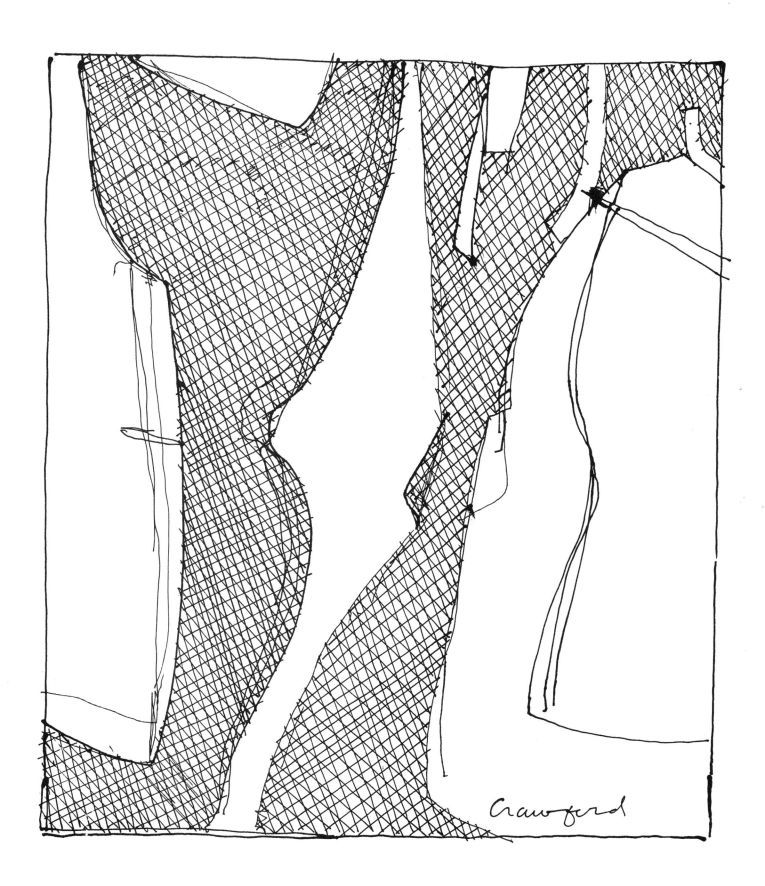

48. *Port Clyde #2, Oct. 21, 1964*

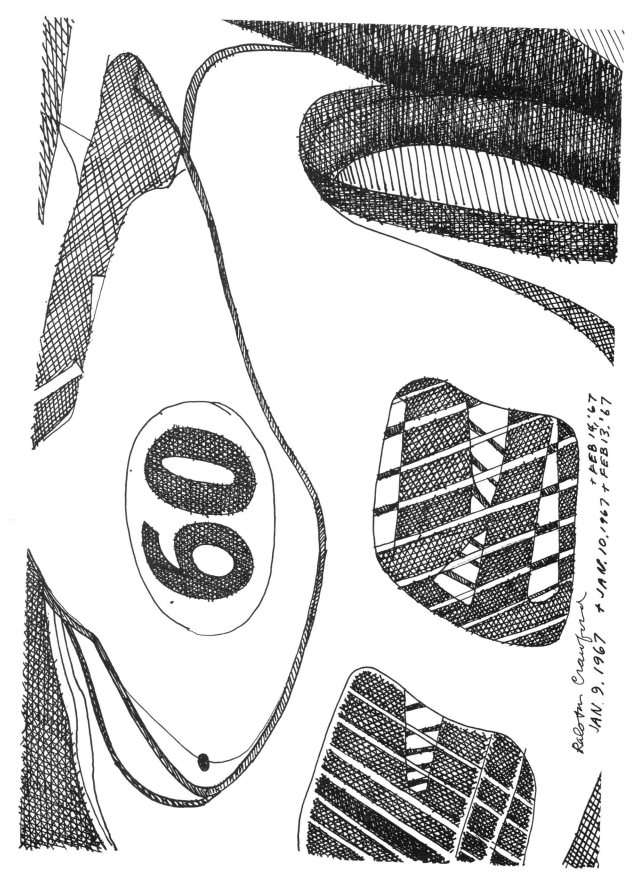

52. *Grand Prix #1, Jan. 9, 10, Feb. 13, 14, 1967*

RALSTON | CRAWFORD

53. *Grand Prix #2, 1968*

54.   *Untitled, Jan. 16, 19, Feb. 14, 1967*

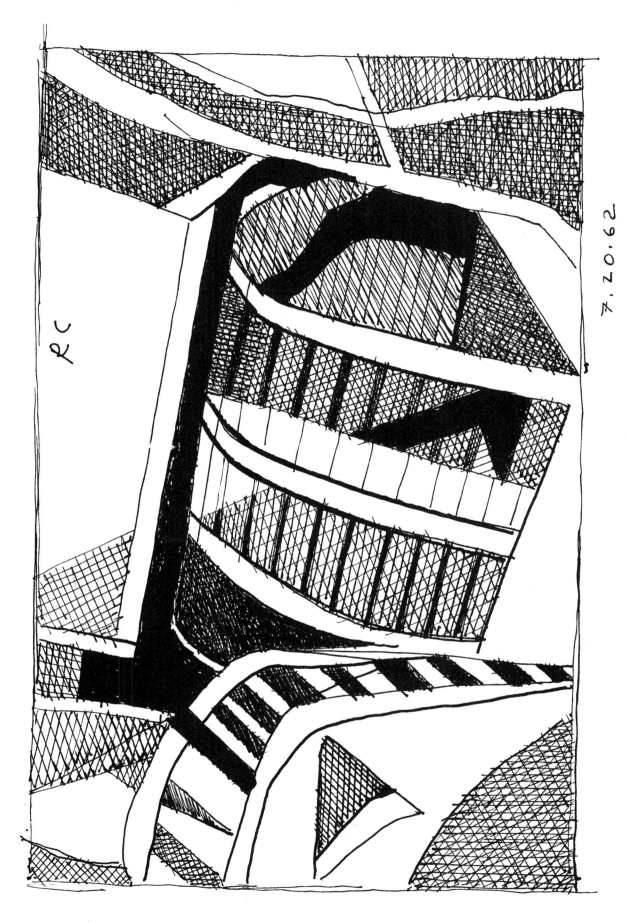

R C

7.20.62

46. *Lobster Pots, July 20, 1962*

49. *Port Clyde #3, Apr. 26, 28, 1965*

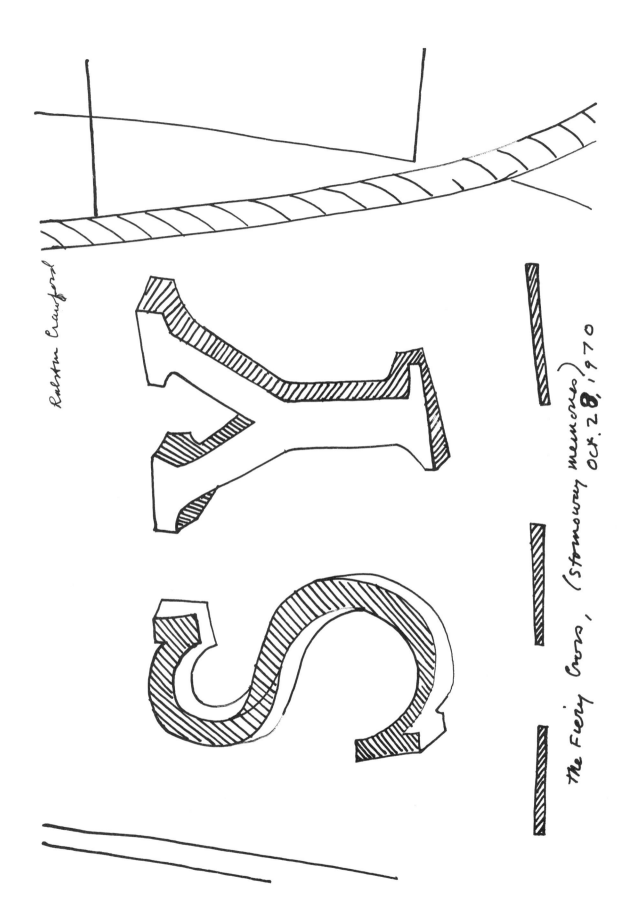

57. *The Fiery Cross (Stornoway Memories), Oct. 28 1970*

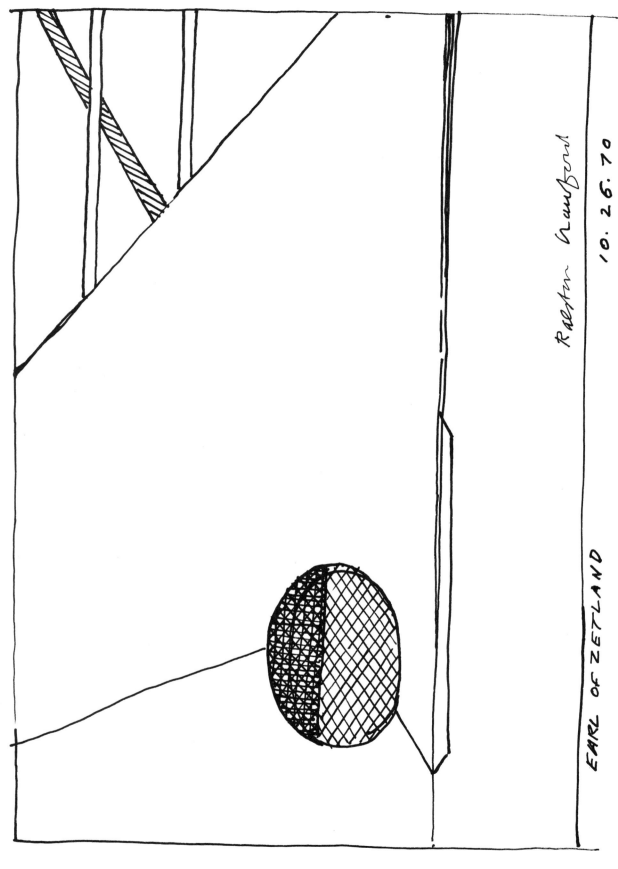

EARL OF ZETLAND

Ralph Lawford

10.26.70

56. *Earl of Zetland, Oct. 26, 1970*

58. *Stornoway (Memories), Oct. 28, Nov. 5, 1970*

Nov. 17, 1970, N. 20' + Nov. 19,

59. *Grand Coulee Feeder Canal, 1970*

R.C. 3.2.72 N.Y.C.
+ Oct. 2 & 1972 N.Y.C.

61. *Penstock Leaves, Coulee Dam, 1973*

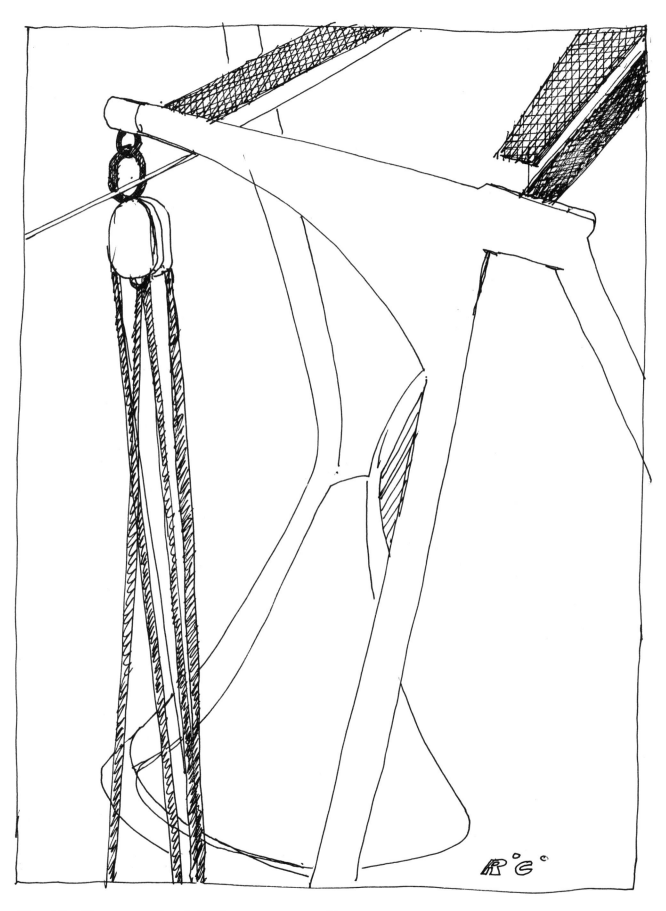

60. *After Stornoway, May 2, 1972*   78

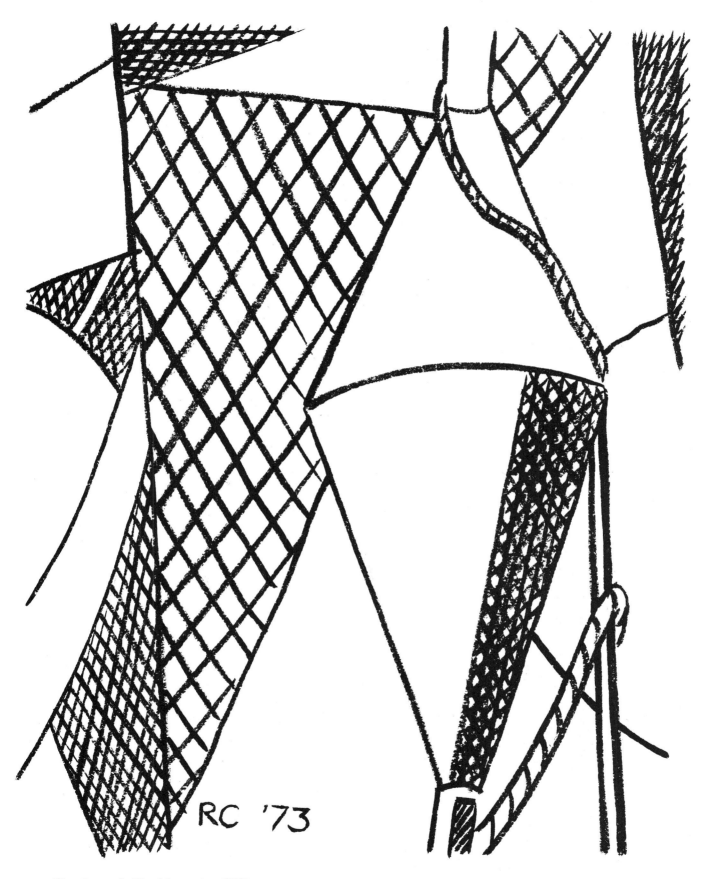

79. *Croix de Vie Memories, 1973*

ONE MAN EXHIBITIONS

1934 Baltimore, Maryland Institute of Arts
1937 Philadelphia, Boyer Galleries
1938 Philadelphia, Philadelphia Art Alliance
1939 New York, Boyer Galleries
1941 Flint (Michigan) Institute of Arts
1944 New York, Downtown Gallery
1946 Santa Barbara Museum
   San Francisco Museum of Art
   Portland (Oregon) Art Museum
   Seattle Art Museum
   New York, Downtown Gallery
1947 Washington, D.C., Howard University
   Honolulu Academy of Arts
1949 Cincinnati Art Museum
   Minneapolis, University of Minnesota
   Jacksonville, Illinois, MacMurray College
1950 New York, Downtown Gallery
   Baton Rouge, Louisiana State University
1952 Hempstead, L. I., N. Y., Hofstra College
1953 Tuscaloosa, University of Alabama
   Orono, University of Maine
1954 New York, Grace Borgenicht Gallery
1955 New York, E. Weyhe Gallery
   Grace Borgenicht Gallery
   Durham, N.C., Duke University

1956 Cincinnati, Contemporary Arts Center
   New York, Grace Borgenicht Gallery
1957 Grand Rapids Art Association, Michigan
   Middletown, Conn., Wesleyan University
1958 Memphis, Brooks Memorial Gallery
   London, England, St. George's Gallery Prints
   Milwaukee Art Center
1960 Cincinnati, A. B. Closson Company
1961 Lexington, University of Kentucky
   San Francisco Museum of Art
   Lincoln, University of Nebraska
   Rochester, Michigan, Oakland University
   Middletown, Conn., Wesleyan University
   New York, Lee Nordness Gallery
   Duluth, University of Minnesota
1962 Orono, University of Maine
1963 Montgomery Museum of Fine Arts, Alabama
1966 Champaign, University of Illinois
1968 Omaha, Creighton University
1969 New Orleans, Bienville Gallery
1971 New York, Zabriskie Gallery
   Lee Nordness Gallery
   St. Louis, Helman Gallery
1973 New Orleans, Bienville Gallery
   Lexington, University of Kentucky
   New York, Zabriskie Gallery
   Washington, D.C., National Collection of
   Fine Arts, Smithsonian Institution

WATERCOLORS

62. MAITLAND BRIDGE 1938
   Pen and brush 8½ x 10½   p. 34
   Lent by Lynn Springer, St. Louis, Mo.

63. PAWN SHOP, THIRD AVENUE #2 1939
   Pen and brush 10 x 14   p. 82

64. POYDRAS STREET COFFEE WHARF,
   NEW ORLEANS 1939
   Pen and brush 9⅞ x 16   p. 83

65. ANCHOR 1939
   Pen and brush 11 x 15½   p. 84

66. SANFORD TANKS 1940
   Pen and brush 16 x 12   p. 85

67. BLUE AND WHITE 1945
   Brush   15 x 20   p. 87

68. PLANE CRASH c. 1945
   Brush 14½ x 11   p. 86

69. BIKINI 1946
   Gouache 12½ x 16¾   p. 89
   Lent by Charles Simon, New York, N.Y.

70. WHARF OBJECTS AT
   SANTA BARBARA #2 1948
   Gouache 13½ x 20   p. 88
   Lent by Mr. & Mrs. Livingston Goddard,
   Fairfax, Va.

71. S.S. DE GRASSE 1952
   Gouache 7¼ x 10¾   p. 92

72. COLOGNE #1 1952
   Gouache 18¼ x 11½   p. 90

73. THIRD AVENUE ELEVATED 1952
   Gouache 11 x 7¼   p. 91

74. HARBOUR SCENE 1952
   Gouache 11 x 15   p. 93

75. BIKINI 1952
   Gouache 15 x 11   p. 94

76. NEW ORLEANS CEMETERY 1953
   Gouache 10 x 14   p. 95

77. DEAD TORO, DEAD HORSE 1963 ?
   Gouache 12⅛ x 19¾   p. 96
   Private Collection, Lexington, Ky.

78. LOS PENITENTES 1973
   Gouache 11 x 8½   p. 81

79. CROIX DE VIE MEMORIES 1973
   Gouache 15¼ x 11½   p. 79

78. *Los Penitentes, 1973*

63. *Pawn Shop, Third Avenue #2, 1939*

RALSTON CRAWFORD, 1939

64. *Poydras Street Coffee Wharf, New Orleans, 1939*

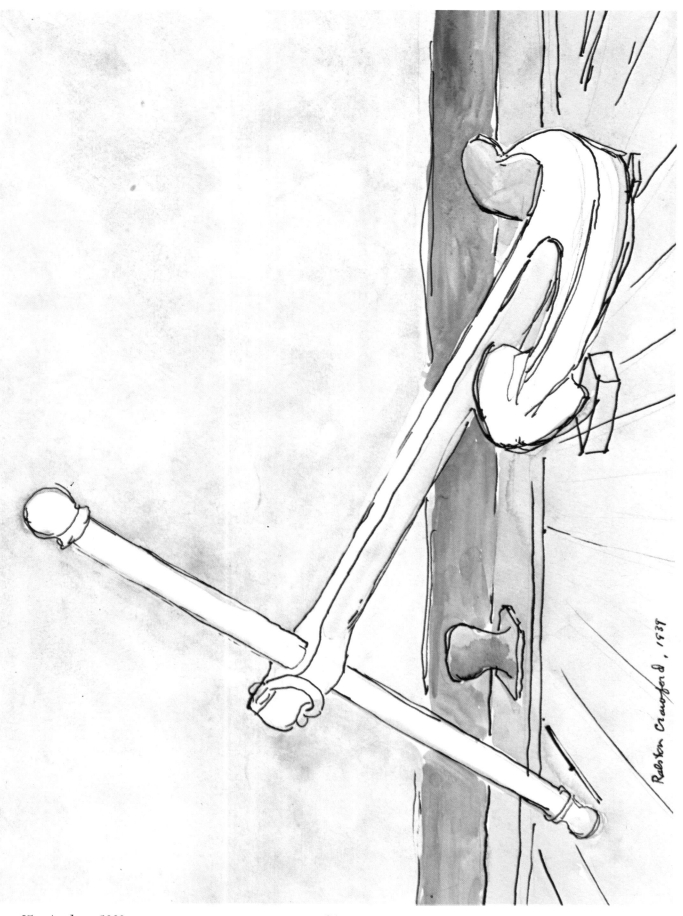

65. *Anchor, 1939*

66. *Sanford Tanks, 1940*

68. *Plane Crash, c. 1945*

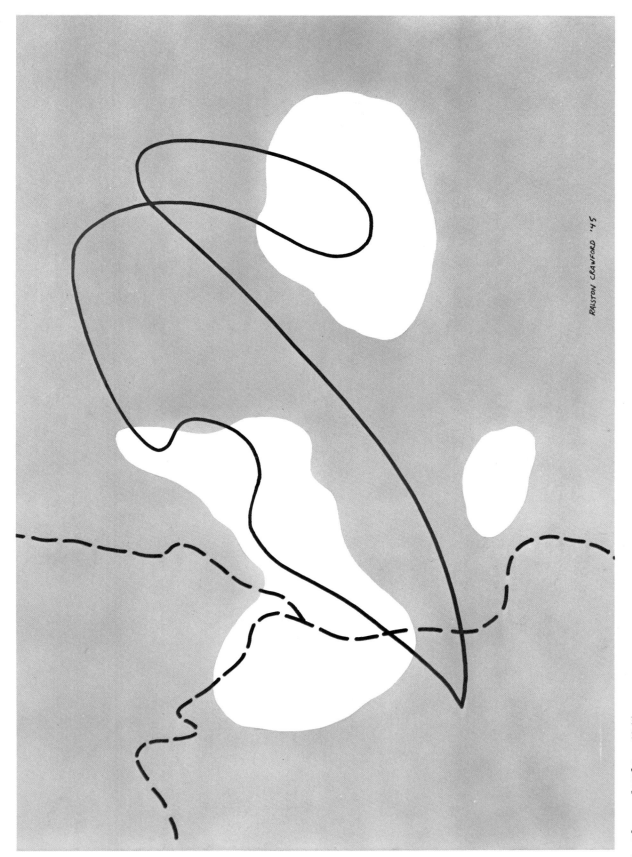

67. *Blue and White, 1945*

70. *Wharf Objects at Santa Barbara #2, 1948*

69. Bikini, 1946

RALSTON CRAWFORD

72. *Cologne #1, c. 1952*

73. *Third Avenue Elevated, 1952*

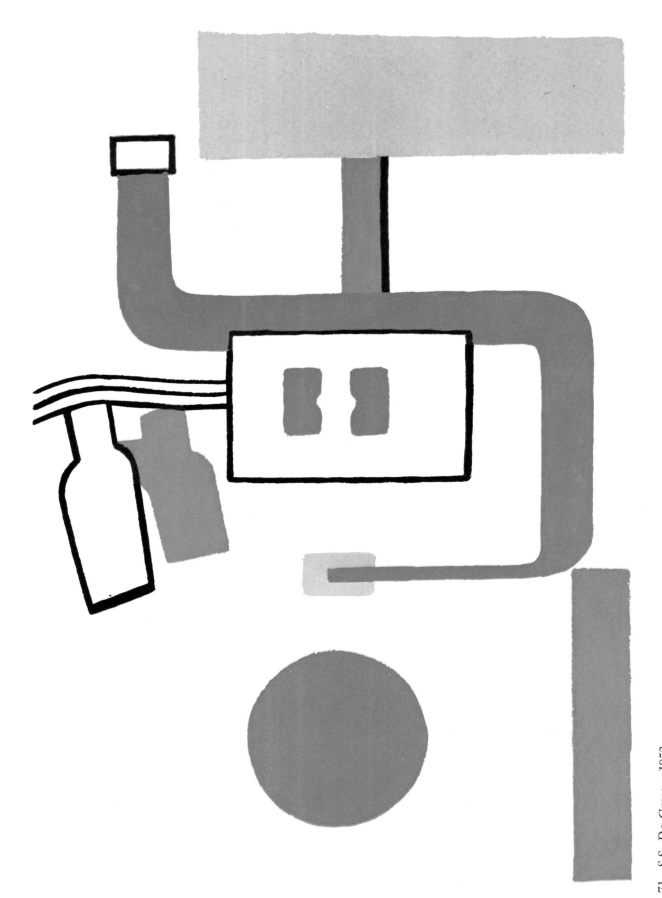

71. S.S. De Grasse, 1952

RALSTON CRAWFORD OCT. 23/28, '52

74. *Harbour Scene, 1952*

75. *Bikini, 1952*

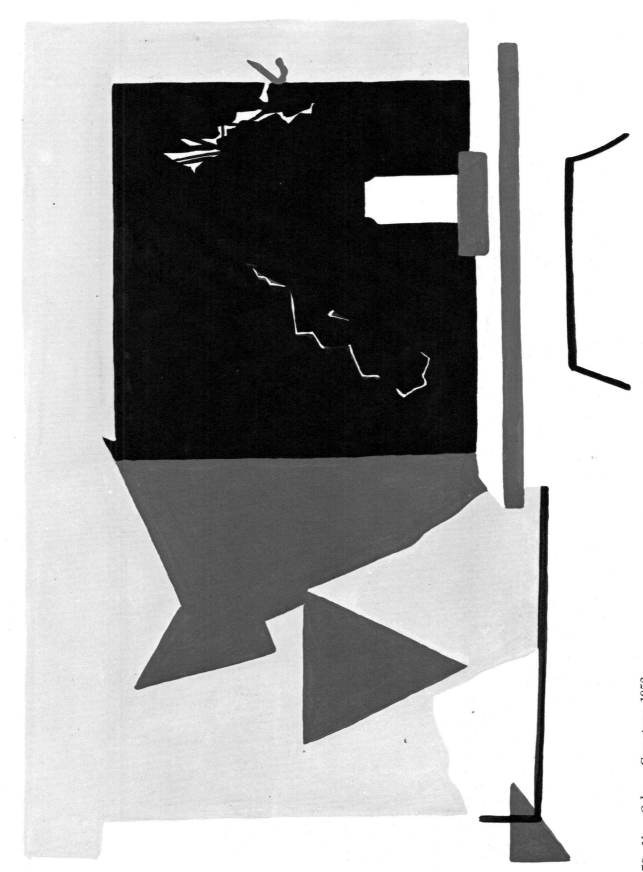

76. *New Orleans Cemetery, 1953*

RALSTON CRAWFORD

77. *Dead Toro, Dead Horse, 1963* ?